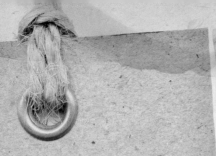

WELCOME
TO OUR 40th BIRTHDAY PARTY.

It's four decades since the original Browns opened in Brighton and we're celebrating in style. We're certainly not suffering any mid-life crisis. Browns knows what it does best – ensuring our loyal customers have a great time. Thanks to fine, affordable food and drink and attentive service. That remains our aim.

Not that we are resting on our laurels. To survive in the often fickle restaurant world you have to keep moving forward. The opening of our new Liverpool offshoot in 2013 brings the total number of Browns Bar & Brasseries to 28. Each one with its own individual character, often set in buildings of remarkable splendour. It pleases us when a happy customer tells staff: *"We didn't realise you were a chain!"*

Chain we are – but one that has a deep responsibility to its legacy. We feel we've shaped the way the British dine out or meet up for a drink. Turn the pages of this celebratory book and take a trip down a culinary Memory Lane. Trace the way we've all changed since those distant days of 1973. Oh and get ready to party. We've always done parties exceptionally well. Grab one of our classic cocktails, order some food to share and settle in the booth under the Big Clock.

HERE'S TO THE NEXT 40 YEARS. CHEERS!

BROWNS LEGACY

NINETEEN SEVENTY THREE

Very different times. Margaret Thatcher, then Education Secretary, tells a BBC audience of children: *"I don't think there will be a woman Prime Minister in my lifetime"*, while Manchester United are en route to relegation and still two decades away from winning a league title.

Some things bizarrely don't change – David Bowie is hot pop news then as now. I can imagine quite a few Ziggy wannabes queuing to get into the hip new eaterie launched in Brighton that year.

Browns was the name. Hardly a glam monicker, but the time and place were perfect for a breath of bracing fresh air in the staid world of British catering. Forty years on, that Browns legacy is going from strength to strength across 28 locations. The trademark Big Clock ticks on as an enduring guarantee of a good time.

In 1973 £10,000 bought you a lot – a restaurant at a pinch. Still it was an act of courage for founders Jeremy Mogford and John Mayhew to borrow that sum, half from family, half from the bank, to set up a 60-seater eaterie in such difficult times. Industrial turmoil and the Oil Crisis culminated by the year's end in the introduction of a Three Day Week, rationing electricity.

COQ AU VIN, SALAD, JACKET 75p

ON BLACKBOARD AT BRIGHTON, 1973

"I like wandering up St Giles to immerse myself in the busy conviviality of Browns Restaurant – a wonderful, friendly place where, perhaps uniquely in Britain, you can get an excellent Caesar Salad and a bacon cheeseburger without having to sit among pounding music and a lot of ersatz Route 66 signs."

BILL BRYSON
NOTES FROM A SMALL ISLAND

THE LONDON BROWNS have always shared a metropolitan glamour. The COVENT GARDEN branch, a gloriously converted courthouse, is on St Martin's Lane in the heart of theatreland. In different times, after the Apollo shows finished folk used to flock over because it was the only place open. Licensing laws meant you couldn't drink without food in the evenings, so everyone used to come in and order a last minute meal. You only got a table if you ate, so chef **MARCO PIERRE WHITE** dropping in for coffee, would tip the hostess £20 each time to secure one.

FORTUNATELY BROWNS WAS a huge hit from Day One. A mood lightener. A game changer. The queues stretched round the block. The cafe bar formula was simple: **FEISTY WAITRESSES, CHOSEN FOR LOOKS AND PERSONALITY,** serving bistro staples and cocktails to a wide range of clientele in a mix and match colonial-style setting. It might sound familiar now, but back then it was revolutionary – based on the SPAGHETTI FACTORY cafe in Vancouver and JOE ALLEN'S in London.

MOGFORD and MAYHEW did most of the building work themselves, restoring an old building society branch in the famous Lanes quarter. Having splashed out on potted kentia palms, over mantel mirrors, swan neck wall lamps, bentwood chairs, hanging baskets and, of course, the **BIG CLOCK**, they couldn't run to a deep fat frier. So the spud offering was jackets. Floury and fluffy from the convector microwave. Chips only made their bow after BROWNS expanded into its second location, in Oxford in 1976.

For a quid you could have spaghetti with a choice of four sauces (meat, tomato, seafood and mushroom), garlic bread and a side salad. **SECOND HELPINGS WERE FREE**. Hot sandwiches included club, pastrami, and VERA's double egg and bacon; salad choice was vegetarian, tuna, chef's ham and chicken.

Typical mains were sirloin steak, grilled mixed fish (trout, red mullet and whitebait), rack of lamb and PEASANT'S POT (a MOGFORD family recipe featuring pork and beans). All served with a jacket potato (butter or sour cream) and mixed salad. Puddings stuck to chocolate cake, cheesecake and apple pie. Coffee came from **ONE OF THE FIRST ESPRESSO MACHINES** and ice cream milkshakes were a draw.

There were also daily specials chalked up. *"We'd only make perhaps three portions. You had a blackboard, put Sold Out next to it. Customers would think 'Those are popular, must get here earlier next time,'* recalls JEREMY MOGFORD. *"The arrival of an Indonesian chef broadened culinary horizons. He did this dish of chicken, beansprouts, eggs and rice. He called it Nasi Indonese. Very exotic, a great favourite.*

"Eighties house red was from France, but originally we went to a warehouse in Sussex, which imported red wine concentrate and they'd mix it with water according to our needs. 75p a bottle when we started. To beat strict licensing laws wine was served out of a teapot. There was no separate bar. We shut one afternoon a week and were closed on Sundays, of course. Nobody would have come if we had tried to open."

Loud music, table sharing and **STAFF ORIGINALLY ALLOWED TO SMOKE** while serving restored the cool factor. Current Brighton general manager Julia "Jules" Clark, who first worked there as a waitress in the late Eighties, recalls: *"It still had original wooden flooring, no high chairs, no starters, just garlic bread. It was all geared to students.* **IT WAS ROCK AND ROLL.** *Waitresses wore short black skirts, DMs, but their own choice of tie. The girls looked like* **EXTRAS FROM** *a Robert Palmer video, you know,* **ADDICTED TO LOVE**.

"IT WAS SUCH A COOL PLACE TO WORK. *They used to hire a lot of girls from the art college.* **YOU HAD TO LOOK GOOD.** *It was interesting for people watching. I remember once being late for work and climbing up to alter the big clock you get in all Browns and smashing it. It had to be repaired. No one grassed on me. We were close."*

In the early Nineties a band calling themselves On A Friday played the Jericho Tavern, Oxford not far from Browns in Oxford, where their lead guitarist, Ed O'Brien worked as a barman alongside me. I was a keen photographer and took the first ever publicity shots. Soon after EMI signed them and changed their name to **RADIOHEAD**. The rest is history, as they say.

- Rupert Elvin, Browns Oxford

The founders didn't envisage a chain as such, but it was inevitable. Mayhew left amicably after they expanded into Cambridge in 1987, setting a template for branches in affluent university cities (Bristol followed in 1982) followed inexorably by entry into the London market. When Bass bought the chain on January 1 1998, several further Browns were in the development stage. Deeper pockets were needed to transform the concept into what it is today. A wider-ranging all-day menu and with a concentration on cocktails in an expanded drinks offering. The key for current owners Mitchells & Butlers has been not to sacrifice the much-loved Browns identity.

Vermont-born Sarah Fox joined in 1998, having lived next door to the Cambridge Browns as a student, and has managed both Edinburgh and Glasgow. She knows her market: *"Edinburgh ticks all the boxes – university, shopping, the festival, a cluster of places to eat and drink. Browns' secret there and elsewhere is we take care of people. There's a sense of belonging people have – those who work there and those who become our regular customers, succeeding generations often. In terms of working, I love it because people love it. We're part of a big chain, but* **THE HEART OF WHAT WE DO IS STILL THE SAME AS IN THE EARLY DAYS**. *To create a menu and a brand you have to have consistency."*

That just about sums up the Browns Legacy.
www.browns-restaurants.co.uk/home

the nineteen 70s

Browns
RESTAURANT & COFFEE HOUSE

Slade
are the Christmas no.1 with "Merry Xmas Everybody"

MUSICAL accompaniment

David Bowie 'retires' Ziggy Stardust at the Hammersmith Odeon

The charts are dominated by Glam Rock with **T. Rex**, **The Sweet**, Suzi Quatro, Gary Glitter, Mott the Hoople, Wizzard, Alvin Stardust and **Mud** on Top of the Pops

Album releases

Pink Floyd
The Dark Side of the Moon
Mike Oldfield
Tubular Bells
The Who
Quadraphenia
Mott the Hoople
Mott
David Bowie
Aladdin Sane

it all began in 1973

Entrepreneur Jeremy Mogford
opens the first Browns restaurant in Brighton in 1973 with an investment of £10,000

HELLO world!

Beverley Knight, Kate Thornton, Peter Andre, Jack Davenport, Adrien Brody, Noel Fielding, Dermot O'Leary, Rufus Wainwright, Kate Beckinsale, Leigh Francis (Keith Lemon)

Sporting Life

Sunderland AFC defeat Leeds United A.F.C. to win the FA Cup final.

Red Rum wins his first Grand National.

Billie Jean King picks up her 5th Wimbledon Women's single title.

Red Rum

The Exorcist, **The Sting**, **American Graffiti**, Last Tango in Paris, Jesus Christ Superstar and **Live and Let Die** were all on the...

SILVER SCREEN

FASHION STATEMENTS

Platform shoes get higher and flares get

wider...for men as well as women...

drive - in

N THE NEWS

US troops withdraw om Vietnam, Britain joins the mon Market, Sydney Opera House ened by Elizabeth II, Princess Anne marries Captain Mark Phillips

Debuts on the Box

Last of the Summer Wine
The Wombles, That's Life!
The World at War

Prawn Cocktail

40 white tiger prawns (10 each)
8 iceberg lettuce leaves (2 each)
4 lemon wedges
200g cocktail sauce
16 small triangles of wholemeal
bread, *spread with butter*
120g dried cherry tomatoes
20g fresh horseradish
4 sprigs of flat leaf parsley
8 red chicory leaves (2 each)
8 white chicory leaves (2 each)
20ml extra virgin olive oil
200g mayonnaise
60g tomato sauce
20g horseradish sauce
*Dash each with Worcester sauce,
brandy and Tabasco
Salt and pepper to taste*

Place all the ingredients in a bowl and mix together. Serve in individual glasses

1973 DINNER PARTY FAVOURITES

HEPHERD'S PIE

FILLING

500g lamb mince
120g diced celery
100g sliced leeks
100g diced onions
20g rosemary
300ml red wine
100g flour
100g peas
50g tomato paste
600ml lamb (or other meat) stock
100g tinned chopped tomatoes
20ml Worcester sauce

SWEET POTATO MASH TOPPING

4-5 sweet potatoes
3 cloves garlic, minced
Seasoning and butter as required

First prepare sweet potato mash for topping. Peel and cube the sweet potatoes. Steam for 15-20 minutes until soft, then mash with garlic, butter and seasoning.

To prepare filling add red wine to boiling stock and simmer for 10 minutes to reduce alcohol. Heat some oil in a large saucepan, add the mince and begin to cook, breaking it up to ensure no lumps. When all the mince is coloured, drain it in a large colander to remove fat and return it to the pan.

Add the onions, carrots, celery, peas and leeks and sweat them until softened, then add the flour and tomato paste, season and stir until coated evenly. Cook for 2-3 minutes. Add the chopped tomatoes, rosemary and the boiling lamb stock, turn heat down and simmer until meat is tender (approx 30-40 minutes). Finally add the Worcester sauce and check seasoning. Cook for a further five minutes, then split the mix into four pie dishes, top with the sweet potato mash and serve with green beans or creamed spinach.

PROFITEROLES

CHOUX PASTRY

60g strong plain flour
150ml cold water
2 large eggs, beaten
50g butter

300ml whipping cream
400g chocolate (melted)
Icing sugar to taste
Sprigs of mint

Sieve flour with a teaspoon of sugar into a jug. Melt the butter with the cold water in a pan over a medium heat. Bring to the boil and immediately take off the heat.

Add the flour mix all in one go, quickly beating it to a smooth dry ball. Add the eggs, bit by bit, mixing thoroughly with every addition, until the mixture looks like a glossy paste. Grease a baking sheet and rinse under the cold tap. Shake off the excess water. Dollop the mixture on to the sheet in one teaspoon measures and bake on a high shelf at 200°C/gas 5 for 10 minutes. Turn up the heat to 220°C/gas 6 and cook for another 10-15 mins. Don't open the oven!

When baked the individual profiteroles will swell. Turn on to a cooling rack and pierce the side of each profiterole to cool. Beat your whipped cream with a little icing sugar and pipe into your choux buns once cool. Pour over chocolate sauce and serve with dusting of icing sugar and spring of mint.

Hemingway Martini

"Shaken not stirred" is James Bond's much-quoted Martini dictum. We prefer Ernest Hemingway's celebration in A Farewell To Arms: "I had never tasted anything so cool and clean... they made me feel civilised.." That's why our cocktail recommendations kick off with a trio of classic Martini variants, including naturally....The Hemingway.

The great writer loved vermouth. While recuperating from his wounds during World War I, he would ask friends to smuggle bottles of it into his hospital room. He liked his cocktails, cold, too, For his Martinis he froze the glass "so cold you can't hold it in your hand, it sticks to the fingers."

75ml Tanqueray 10
12.5ml Noilly Prat

Pour Noilly Prat over cubed ice and stir 12 times clockwise and 12 times anti-clockwise.

Once the ice cubes are well coated pour out all excess liquid.
Add the gin and repeat, 12 times clockwise, 12 times anti-clockwise.
Quickly fine strain into a chilled Martini glass.
Garnish with an olive on a stick.

Vesper Martini

Back to 007. My name is Vesper...Vesper Martini. Invented and named (after Bond girl Vesper Lynd) by our hero in the 1953 novel, Casino Royale, it originally consisted of gin and vodka with Kina Lillet – for which, in our Browns version, we substitute Noilly Prat. In the 2008 film, Quantum Of Solace, Bond sinks six of them.

50ml Sipsmith Gin
17.5ml Sipsmith Vodka
7.5ml Noilly Prat

Shake all ingredients with cubed ice. Fine strain into a chilled Martini glass. Garnish with a lemon twist.

BROWNS GIMLET

Gimlets traditionally match gin with lime juice. In the Browns Gimlet we pursue an innovative shortcut, combining aromatic elderflower cordial with Tanqueray's Rangpur Gin, whose botanicals include the Rangpur lime, a citrus fruit that is not a true lime but a hybrid between a lemon and a mandarin orange. Result: a uniquely refreshing flavour surge.

75ml Rangpur Gin
15ml elderflower cordial
Dash bitters

Shake and double strain into a chilled Martini glass. Garnish with a lime twist.

SAN FRANCISCO and NEW YORK

have laid strong claims to the origin of the Martini. Numerous similar cocktail recipes appeared in late 19th century bartending guides.

It was certainly Prohibition and the relative ease of illegal gin manufacture that led to the Martini's rise as the predominant US cocktail of the mid 20th century. With the repeal of Prohibition, and the ready availability of quality gin, the drink became progressively drier.

Let another great writer, James Thurber have the last word: "One Martini is all right. Two are too many, and three are not enough."

YOU'VE BEEN WARNED!

One Flew over *The Cuckoo's Nest*, *The Rocky Horror Picture Show*, The Who's Tommy and *Jaws* were all on the...

SILVER SCREEN

LIVING IN... 1975

Graduating to pastures new.

The phenomenal success of Brighton has Browns plotting a second outlet in Oxford – somewhere cool to celebrate passing those finals.

Sporting Life

Muhammad Ali defeats **Joe Frazier** in the 'Thrilla in Manilla'. **Derby County** win the Division 1 title for the second time in four seasons. **Niki Lauda** becomes Formula 1 World Drivers' Champion.

HELLO WORLD

David Beckham
will.i.am *(Black Eyed Peas)*,
Melanie Brown *(Mel B)*,
Russell Brand, Angelina Jolie,
Curtis Jackson *(50 Cent)*,
Michael Bublé, Kate Winslet, Tiger Woods

Debuts on the Box

The Sweeney
Fawlty Towers
The Good Life
Space 1999

IN THE news

NASA launches the Viking 1 planetary probe toward Mars

Bill Gates and Paul Allen found **Microsoft** in Albuquerque, New Mexico. **British Leyland** comes under Government control. **Charlie Chaplin knighted.** The Vietnam War ends as Communist forces from North Vietnam take Saigon.

MUSICAL accompaniment

The Sex Pistols play their first concert at St. Martin's School of Art in London

Album releases

David Bowie
Young Americans

Rod Stewart
Atlantic Crossing

Elton John
Captain Fantastic and the Brown Dirt Cowboy

Bruce Springsteen
Born to Run

Queen release **Bohemian Rhapsody**, which spends 9 weeks at the top spot and is the Christmas no.1

High waisted baggy jeans and trousers for both sexes are the latest **fashion statement**, as are platform shoes and clogs. Girls were loving the 30's and 40's look with **bright heavy make up and big lashes**, the three piece suit was back for men.

13

GARLIC BREAD

Garlic bulb
7g salt
40ml oil
350ml water
550g strong plain white flour
10g dried yeast
Semolina and herbs for dusting

Baking's all the rage, so why not create your garlic bread from scratch. Alternatively, fill a bought-in baguette with garlic butter (see at the end).

Roast the whole garlic bulb in oven until soft, cool and pop the cloves out of the skin. Put flour in bowl, salt on one side, yeast on other. Add liquid and mix with hands until thoroughly combined. Tip on to a floured board and knead for eight minutes. Leave to rise in a plastic bowl with plastic bag over in a cool area for two hours. Take out and knock bag. Fold in your already roasted garlic, chopped. Shape and leave to prove for one hour. Re-shape, dust and cook for 14 minutes 220°C/gas 7.

Short-cut

Mash together eight cloves garlic, a handful of finely chopped parsley, 125g butter with a pinch of salt. Cut half way into a bought in baguette at 3cm intervals, taking care not to slice through. Spoon in blobs of the butter mix. Wrap in foil and bake in oven at 220°C/gas 7 for 20 minutes. Unwrap and serve.

Witch SOLE

4 whole witch soles
(plaice or lemon sole are suitable alternatives)
400g caperberries, drained
250g butter
4 lemons
4 finely diced shallots
Good handful chopped parsley
200g brown shrimp

Ask your fishmonger to remove head, black skin and skirt. With a sharp knife ease back the flesh from the backbone to leave a small pocket (approx 1in by 3in).

Season fish and place on a greased tray and lightly grill for five minutes. While grilling the fish, place a shallow pan on a low heat to get hot. When the fish is cooked, the pan should be hot, add the caperberries, shrimps and shallots.

Add the butter, and let it reach a nut brown colour. When this occurs add the parsley and the juice of half a lemon, remove from heat immediately, season with salt and pepper. Pour over cooked fish and serve with the remaining lemon half.

Serve with a side of avocado and bacon salad.

ser
4

Black Forest Trifle

100g chocolate brownie,
broken into pieces

350g custard

240g blackberries,
soaked in kirsch

120g whipped cream
(with 4tbsp of icing sugar
whipped into it)

Chocolate shavings and mint
sprigs to garnish

1975
DINNER PARTY FAVOURITES

Build ingredients in
four individual glasses,
starting with a dollop
of cream, followed by
brownie, blackberries,
custard, cream topping
and garnish.

FROZEN STRAWBERRY DAIQUIRI

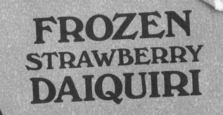

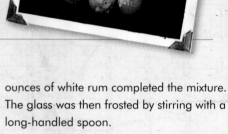

The Daiquiri cocktail family's main ingredients are rum, citrus (typically lime juice) and sugar. The name comes from a beach in Cuba. The drink was supposedly invented by an American mining engineer, named Jennings Cox, who happened to be in Cuba at the time of the Spanish-American War.

Originally the drink was served in a tall glass packed with cracked ice. A teaspoon of sugar was poured over the ice and the juice of one or two limes was squeezed over the sugar. Two or three ounces of white rum completed the mixture. The glass was then frosted by stirring with a long-handled spoon.

The drink gained international popularity in the 1940s, when rum was easier to obtain than other spirits. Hemingway (again – however did he get any writing done?) was a great champion.

Frozen Daiquirís are delicious extensions, mixing rum – and increasingly a choice of other spirits – with pulverised ice and fruit to produce a texture almost like a smoothie and great refreshment value.

Our Browns version combines fresh lime juice with strawberry puree to create just the right sour/sweet balance.

50ml Bacardi Superior Rum
25ml fresh lime juice
20ml strawberry puree
5ml gomme syrup

Blend all ingredients with ice. Garnish with a strawberry or lime wedge.

BACARDI®

ESTD CUBA 1862

'79

HELLO WORLD!

Pete Doherty, Norah Jones, Sophie Ellis-Bextor, James McAvoy, Jonny Wilkinson, Jamie Cullum, Pink, Kelly Brook, Will Young

MUSICAL accompaniment

Madness, The Specials, The Police, The Pretenders and Dire Straits make their chart debuts this year

Album releases

Sister Sledge
We are Family
Abba
Voulez Vous
Michael Jackson
Off The Wall
The Police
Reggatta de Blanc
Gary Numan
The Pleasure Principle

Kate Bush begins her first, and to date, only tour.

The menu moves on...

In the early days there were no starters as such, just garlic bread on offer, a choice of salad dressings, and spuds only came as baked. Now you can have chips and a range of sides, too.

Nottingham Forest F.C. defeat **Malmö FF** 1-0 in the European Cup Final

Seve Ballesteros
wins the **British Open** Golf Tournament

At Wimbledon, **Bjorn Borg** and **Martina Navratilova** are champions

Tales of the Unexpected
Blankety Blank

Antiques Roadshow
Worzel Gummidge
Question Time

debuts
ON THE BOX

18

Sparked by the cinema release of The Who's **Quadraphenia**, a Mod revival reflects in fashion – a reappearance of **sharp 60's style suits, Fred Perry** shirts and fishtail parkas

For her, the fashion statements couldn't be more different – **Disco** is at it's fashion peak, with spandex, lurex and **strappy stilettoes**

Margaret Thatcher becomes the country's first female prime minister. McDonald's introduces the Happy Meal. Sony Walkman goes on sale in Japan. Philips demonstrates compact disc publicly for the first time.

IN THE NEWS
Columbia
the first fully functional Space Shuttle orbiter, is delivered to the John F. Kennedy Space Center

Apocalypse Now, *Alien*, *Kramer vs. Kramer*, The Amityville Horror and The Muppet Movie were all on the...

SILVER SCREEN

Caesar dressing

2 cloves garlic
30g anchovies in oil
2 egg yolks
8g English mustard
1 lemon zest and juice
100ml rapeseed oil
Pinch black pepper
15ml water *(or as required)*

Composed salad

1 cos lettuce
2 little gem lettuces
75g Parmigiano Reggiano cheese
75g croutons
50g anchovies *(drained weight)*

Classic Caesar SALAD

Remove the stalk from the cos lettuce, tear into small bite-size pieces, then break the gems into individual leaves, then divide into four portions.

To make Caesar dressing place all ingredients, except the oil, into a container and blitz until smooth, slowly add the rapeseed oil until completely incorporated. Check seasoning. Pour over lettuce and mix in croutons and shaved Parmigiano Reggiano (parmesan).

serves 4

'79 Dinner Party Favourites

Coq au vin

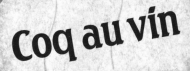

The marinade

450ml red wine
15g redcurrant jelly
15g chopped onions
100g chopped celery
100g chopped carrot
4 cloves peeled garlic
3g thyme
4 bayleaves

Four large chicken pieces

100ml olive oil
40g flour
100g diced pancetta
300g silver skin onions
200g button mushrooms, *quartered*
80ml kitchen brandy
800g mashed potato
40g unsalted butter
250g green beans
Parsley for garnish

Place chicken pieces and marinade components in a roasting tray and leave for a minimum of four hours, then remove the chicken.

Brown the chicken on all sides in oil until golden brown, remove from the pan, add the pancetta, silver skin onions and button mushrooms and fry in the chicken juices until golden. Return the chicken to the pan, dust with the flour and stir well, then add brandy and cook for two minutes. Sieve the marinade over the chicken, ensuring the chicken is fully covered in the liquid.

Cover the pan and simmer for 1-1½ hours, adding a small amount of chicken stock, if necessary. Serve with sauce ladled over, accompanied by the mash and green beans. Peas, leeks and bacon makes a great side.

Creme Caramel

The caramel

160g sugar

The custard

4 free range eggs
1tsp vanilla extract
25g caster sugar
600ml full-fat milk

Unsalted butter, for greasing the ramekins

Pre-heat oven to 150°C/gas 2. Warm the ramekins in the oven. Pour the sugar and six tablespoons of water into a pan. Dissolve the sugar slowly then boil till the sugar turns a deep colour. Remove immediately from the heat and pour the caramel into the warmed ramekins.

Set aside to cool and become hard. Once hard, butter the sides of the ramekins above the level of the caramel. Whisk the eggs, vanilla extract and caster sugar together in a bowl. Pour the milk into a saucepan, gently heat over a low heat, then strain the milk through a fine sieve on to the egg mixture in the bowl.

Whisk together until smooth, then pour the mixture into the prepared ramekins. Stand the ramekins in a roasting tin and fill the tin half-way with boiling water from a kettle. Cook in the oven for about 20-30 minutes or until the custard has set.

Take the crème caramels out of the oven set on a cooling rack. When cool, transfer to the fridge overnight so that the caramel is absorbed into the custard. To serve, loosen the sides of the custard by tipping the ramekin and loosen with a small palette knife round the edges. Place a serving dish on top of the ramekin and turn upside down. Serve.

Piña Colada

BACARDI
ESTD CUBA 1862

Pina Colada in Spanish means Piña (pineapple) and Colada (strained). Coconut, rum, ice and, in the Browns version, double cream, complete the perfect comfort cocktail.

The Piña Colada has been the official beverage of Puerto Rico since 1978. Back in 1974 the management at the Caribe Hilton's Beachcomber Bar in capital San Juan commissioned a signature drink from bartender "Monchito" and, after three months' shaker-driven experimentation, he came up with this perennial favourite.

There's even a song about it, a US no1 hit in the Seventies.

White or dark rum can be used.

At Browns, it has to be Mount Gay, the pride of Barbados.

50ml Mount Gay Rum
50ml pineapple juice
20ml coconut syrup
50ml double cream

Blend ingredients with crushed ice.
Garnish with a pineapple slice.

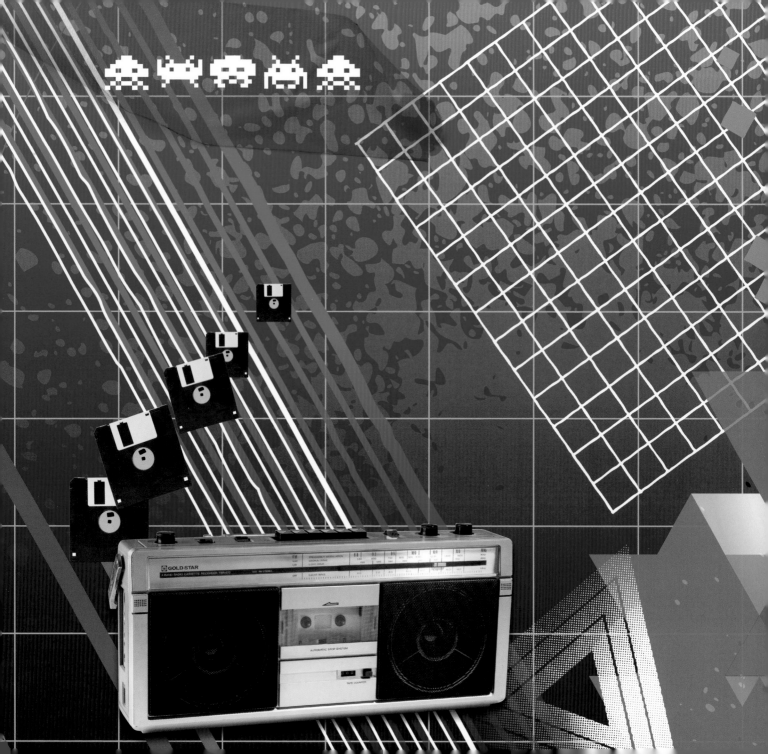

RESTAURANT **Browns** *& BAR*

Almost two decades since Browns was conceived and the two are going strong, sowing the seeds for future habits as many experience their first cappuccino and new world wine in a Browns.

FASHION STATEMENTS FOR BOTH SEXES
The year of legwarmers

FOR HER: Ra Ra skirts and lycra leggings...and...Deelyboppers!
FOR HIM – tight jeans, trainers, active sportswear, designer labels

IN THE NEWS

The **Commodore 64** 8-bit home computer is **launched** by Commodore International. The **first compact discs** appear in music stores in Japan. London's **Barbican Centre opened** by The Queen. 10% of households in the United Kingdom own a **VCR**. The musical **Cats** begins its **18 year Broadway run**. The **Falklands War** begins in April and ends in June with the formal surrender of Argentine forces. **Channel 4** is launched

1982

DEBUTS ON THE BOX
Wogan, Saturday Superstore, 'Allo 'Allo, The Young Ones, **Brookside** and **The Tube**

SPORTING LIFE

Aston Villa win the **European Cup**, beating Bayern Munich 1–0. The 12th FIFA **World Cup** is held in Spain and **won by Italy**. **Larry Holmes** defeats Gerry Cooney for the WBC Heavyweight title. At Wimbledon, **Jimmy Connors** and **Martina Navratilova** are champions

Tootsie, E.T. An Officer and a Gentleman, **Poltergeist,** Annie, Ghandi were all

ON THE Silver Screen...

MADONNA's debut single, "EVERYBODY" released

HELLO WORLD!

Prince William
Duke of Cambridge

Catherine
Duchess of Cambridge

Caleb Followill
(Kings of Leon)

Kirsten Dunst

Matt Smith

Nicki Minaj

Seth Rogen

Andy Roddick

MUSICAL accompaniment

ABC
The Lexicon of Love

YAZOO
Upstairs at Erics

DEXY'S MIDNIGHT RUNNERS
Too-Rye-Ay

KATE BUSH
The Dreaming

CULTURE CLUB
Kissing to be Clever

PHIL COLLINS
Hello, I must be going!

MICHAEL JACKSON
Thriller

Other **top selling chart bands** include: Musical Youth, **Haircut 100,** Duran Duran, **The Human League,** Soft Cell and **Wham!**

‹ 27 ›

LEEKS
vinaigrette

4 long leeks
50ml olive oil
1tbsp red wine vinegar
1tsp Dijon mustard
Freshly ground salt and pepper
Poached egg, to serve

Clean and trim the leeks.
Place in a pan of boiling water and reduce
heat to simmer for 8-10 minutes.
Drain and put in an ice bath. Tip the bowl of the
ice bath so the water runs
out while you prepare the vinaigrette.
Mix all the vinaigrette ingredients
together and pour over the (drained) leeks.
Cover with cling film and put in the
fridge to marinate for a minimum of 2 hours,
maximum 3 days.
When ready to serve, bring to room temperature
and, if you wish, top with a poached egg.

1982
DINNER PARTY FAVOURITES

SWEET CURED GAMMON
with buttered mash and parsley sauce

750g sweetcure gammon joint
(cut in 5mm thick slices)
900g mashed potato
100g unsalted butter
Parsley to garnish

Parsley sauce (makes 200ml)
100ml stock
(juices from the gammon pan)
15g unsalted butter
50g plain flour
100ml milk
Splash double cream
Good handful of finely
chopped parsley

Pot roast the gammon *(this can be done the day before)*. Soften a chopped onion with thyme and parsley in a large lidded, heavy base pan, add 400ml of water and bring to the boil. Put the gammon in and cook in the oven at 160°C/gas 3 for 1½ hours. Take the gammon out of the pan, sieve the juices and keep.

To make the parsley sauce, melt the butter in a pan and beat in the flour off the heat to make a classic roux. Bring the milk, cream and gammon stock to the boil in a pan, stirring all the time. Gradually add this liquid to the roux, a little at a time back on the heat, whisking constantly. Continue adding liquid until the sauce will thinly coat the back of a spoon. Stir in the finely chopped parsley towards the end.

Slice the cooked gammon thinly and serve with the butter-enriched mashed potato, smothered in parsley sauce. Accompany with honey roast carrots and parsnips.

ETON Mess

8 meringues (2 each)
500g red cherries in sauce
80g Greek yoghurt
250ml whipping cream
60g clotted cream
40g hazelnuts
60g white chocolate buttons
4 mint sprigs for garnish

Whip the cream into soft peaks, add the clotted cream, whip again until stiff, then fold in the yoghurt. Toast the hazelnuts under the overhead grill and chop finely.

In a bowl break the meringue, then fold in the cream mix, (pitted) cherries with half the white chocolate buttons and half the toasted hazelnuts.

Transfer to a plate and sprinkle with the remaining hazelnuts and buttons, drizzle some red cherry sauce around the plate. Serve garnished with the mint.

Brandy Alexander

Double cream (alongside brandy, obviously) features in our take on the Brandy Alexander, a drink that became popular in the early 20th century. Its origins are unclear but one story has it named after the Russian Tsar, Alexander II.

It got a boost in the 1980s when it featured in Granada TV's adaptation of Brideshead Revisited. More recently, the character, Peggy Olson, shows her cool Manhattan allegiance by ordering it in Mad Men Series One.

The White Creme de Cacao is a clear version of this liqueur. To ensure this the finest, roasted cocoa beans are only distilled and not percolated. It all adds up to a subtle gem of a cocktail.

25ml
of each of the following...

Rumoured to be named after the Russian Tsar, Alexander II

RÉMY MARTIN
FINE CHAMPAGNE COGNAC

**Remy Martin
White Creme de Cacao
Double cream**

Shake all ingredients with cubed ice.
Fine strain into a chilled Martini glass.
Dust with chocolate.

Browns can have its own Boat Race now! Its third restaurant in Cambridge, housed in a former wing of the old Addenbrooke's Hospital, is to open within a year and proves as first class as Oxford.

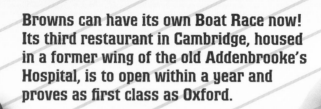

Debuts On The Box

Bread, Beadle's About, Casualty and Lovejoy

In The News

PRINCE ANDREW, Duke of York marries SARAH FERGUSON at Westminster Abbey. DESMOND TUTU becomes the FIRST BLACK ANGLICAN CHURCH BISHOP in South Africa. THE BIG BANG in the London Stock Exchange paves the way for ELECTRONIC TRADING.

SPORTING LIFE

MIKE TYSON wins his first world boxing title in Las Vegas. At Wimbledon, **BORIS BECKER** and Martina Navratilova are champions. **MARADONA'S 'HAND OF GOD'** knocks England out of the World Cup. **ALAIN PROST** wins the Formula One Championship.

fashion statements

MIAMI VICE

FOR HIM: The Crockett & Tubbs look - designer suits, sleeves rolled up, mirror shades, hair gel and designer stubble.

FOR HER: Big hair, shoulder pads, accessories and bags

Hello World!

Alex Turner [Arctic Monkeys]

Mischa Barton

Jamie Bell

Jessica Ennis

Charlotte Church

Lady Gaga

Robert Pattinson

Ellie Goulding

MUSICAL
accompaniment

Pet Shop Boys *Please*
Madonna *Live to Tell*
Beastie Boys *Licensed to Ill*
Queen *A Kind of Magic*
Steve Winwood *Back in the High Life*
Lionel Ritchie *Dancing on the Ceiling*
Bon Jovi *Slippery when Wet*

In the Charts...

PRINCE and the Revolution **KISS**
Robert Palmer *Addicted to Love*
Swing out Sister *Breakout*
Diana Ross *Chain Reaction*

Platoon, **Top Gun**, Crocodile Dundee, The Color of Money, **Ferris Bueller's Day Off** were all on the...

SILVER SCREEN

Crab and Avocado Stack

Cucumber salsa

4 salad potatoes, cooked, skins on
25g cucumber
Handful spring onions
4 cloves prepared garlic
10g capers
10g red and green chillies
Handful of coriander leaves
50ml lime juice and zest
10ml drizzle olive oil
10g caster sugar

300g crab claw meat
25g crème fraiche
5ml English mustard
125g sliced avocado
25ml drizzle balsamic
and olive oil dressing
Small handful baby leaf salad mix
8 crostini sticks

Mix the crab meat, crème fraiche and mustard. To make the salsa, peel and core the cucumber, then finely dice it along with the red & green chillies, spring onion, capers and coriander. Mix together with the oil and lime juice, check taste and add sugar if required. Using a black ring to hold it together, place the avocado at the bottom, top it with the cucumber salsa and finally the crab mix. It should fill the black ring to the top. Serve with the baby leaf salad and crostini sticks.

steak PIE

1986

DINNER PARTY FAVOURITES

‹ 34 ›

500g chuck steak, or even rump
100g diced onion
100g diced carrots
100g diced celery
200g button mushrooms
1 litre 'Maggi' beef bouillon
15ml olive oil
25ml Worcester sauce
350ml Guinness
125ml water
4 bay leaves
25g brown Sugar
300g tomato puree
Puff pastry rolled out to top pie
10g butter
1 egg yolk

STICKY
toffee
pudding

180g pitted dates
240ml water
20g bicarbonate of soda
65g butter (softened)
180g soft light brown sugar
180g self-raising flour
2 eggs
Butter and flour for lining tray
Mint sprigs for garnish

TOFFEE SAUCE
100g demerara sugar
100ml whipping cream
100g butter

Seal the stewing steak in small batches in olive oil. In a large stock pot, fry off the onion, carrot and celery for one minute. Add the sealed stewing steak, then the Guinness, water, Worcester sauce, sugar, bay leaves, tomato puree and bouillon.

Bring to the boil and simmer for approximately one hour. Add the mushrooms and simmer for a further 30 minutes, stirring regularly until the meat is tender but still holds shape. Taste and season with salt and ground black pepper.

To help ensure an even mix of meat and vegetables into each pie, it is advisable to drain the sauce and top up each pie with it.

Place in four individual oval pots or a large sharing dish, top with the puff pastry, brush with egg yolk and bake for 20 minutes at 220C/gas 6. Buttered spring greens goes well with this.

Lightly butter and flour a tray/dish to fit the mixture in. To make the toffee sauce, place the ingredients in a saucepan and bring to the boil. Ensure all sugar is dissolved and well mixed, taking care not to boil over. Cook until a golden colour has been achieved.

Boil the pitted dates with the bicarbonate of soda, remove from the heat, liquidise with a hand blender and cool.

In a bowl mix the softened butter and the sugar and cream until light and fluffy. This will take approximately 8 to 10 minutes. Add the eggs, one by one – mixing evenly each time. Add the liquidised dates, then sieve the flour and stir until smooth and lump-free.

Pour the mix into the prepared tray and bake for 40-50 minutes at 160°C/gas 3 until firm to the touch. Allow to rest and cool for 20 minutes.

Divide into square portions to serve, with clotted cream and drizzled toffee sauce. There should be enough for seconds!

JUST ADD CLOTTED CREAM, POURING CREAM OR CUSTARD TO SUIT

ESPRESSO MARTINI

Maybe not one for the Martini purists, but there's a silky, caffeine kick to this stalwart of the Browns' "Aftertail" list.

The recipe here is for the Classic vodka, Kahlua and cold espresso combo, created in the 1980s – legend has it – by a London cocktail guru late one night for a famous supermodel.

ESPRESSO MARTINI

qually delightful Browns variations include The Italian with Disaronno Amaretto 7.5; The Irish with Baileys & Jameson; The Hazelnut with Frangelico; The Cuban Bacardi 8yr Rum and The Mexican with Patron Anejo & Kahlua.

37.5ml Grey Goose Vodka
12.5ml Kahlua
12.5 gomme syrup
1 shot espresso

Double shake all ingredients with cubed ice. Strain into chilled Martini glass. Garnish with three coffee beans.

1988

THE VARSITY CHALLENGE HOTS UP IN THE CELEB STAKES.

Oxford regulars around this time include Jeremy Irons, Rowan Atkinson (very shy), Tucker from Grange Hill and, naturally, Inspector Morse (John Thaw). Cambridge boast Stephen Fry and Rory McGrath plus sighting of Keanu Reeves.

Browns
RESTAURANT & BAR

In The News...

The Church of England announces that it will allow the ordination of women priests from 1992.

The **first BBC Red Nose Day** raises £15 milli

Margaret Thatcher becomes the **longest serving British prime minister** this century.

The Liberal Democrats are formed.

Benazir Bhutto becomes the first woman Prime Minister of Pakistan.

Hello! magazine launched in the UK

FASHION STATEMENTS

Guys were wearing Hawaiian shirts with leather Aviator jackets, acid washed jeans and shades.

Girls were wearing mini skirts or bleached jeans with Doc Marten shoes or Keds and bomber jackets.

Rihanna, Josh Bowman Rupert Grint, Adele, Tinie Tempah

HELLO WORLD!

Elly Jackson (La Roux) Jessie J, Lacey Turner Tulisa Contostavlos

Rain Man, Die Hard, Who framed Roger Rabbit? and Twins were all on the...

SILVER SCREEN

SPORTING LIFE

Golfer Sandy Lyle becomes the first British winner of the US Masters. **GREAT BRITAIN AND NORTHERN IRELAND WIN 5 GOLD, 10 SILVER AND 9 BRONZE MEDALS AT THE OLYMPICS IN SEOUL.** Ayrton Senna wins the Formula One Championship. Wimbledon beat mighty Liverpool to win the FA Cup.

MUSICAL accompaniment

Prince Lovesexy
Sade Stronger than Pride
Bon Jovi New Jersey
Bros Push
U2 Rattle and Hum

Debuts On The Box...

Red Dwarf, London's Burning, Wheel of Fortune, This Morning, Whose Line Is It Anyway?

IN THE CHARTS...

KYLIE keeps **RICK ASTLEY** off the top spot with her debut single 'I Should Be So Lucky' and **BROS** were very big with their Brosettes!!!

1988

PATE DU MAISON

200g UNSALTED BUTTER, softened
500g CHICKEN LIVERS, trimmed
1 GARLIC clove, chopped
2 sprigs THYME
2 BASIL leaves
3 tbsp PORT
(Cointreau or
Grand Marnier)

Line a terrine mould or ramekins with cling film. Heat one tablespoon of the butter in a frying pan over a medium heat. When the butter is foaming, add the chicken livers. Fry for 1-2 minutes, or until just golden-brown. Add the garlic, thyme, basil and Port. Fry the chicken livers in the mixture for a further 1-2 minutes or until the liquid has evaporated.

Transfer the mixture to a food processor, add the remaining butter and blend to a smooth paste. Season, to taste, with salt and freshly ground black pepper.

Spoon the parfait mixture into the lined terrine or ramekins and chill in the fridge for at leas three hours or until set.

PORK BELLY

with

CREAMEL CABBAGE

4 PORK BELLY PORTIONS, 750g in total
3 ORANGES, zest and juice
150g HONEY
15g GROUND CUMIN
750g SAVOY CABBAGE, shredded
200g SMOKED STREAKY BACON, cut into strips
400ml DOUBLE CREAM
100ml OLIVE OIL
4 BRAEBURN APPLES
75g BUTTER
100g DEMERARA SUGAR
100ml ASPALL'S APPLE BALSAMIC VINEGAR
200g PORK BACK FAT RIND
250ml APPLE BRANDY JUS

Whisk together the orange juice and zest, honey and cumin and coat the pork belly portions evenly with the marinade for three to four hours.

When ready to cook rub the pork belly skin with salt and olive oil. Place on a wire rack in a roasting tin. Roast at 200ºC/gas 6 for 30 minutes.

Turn down to 180ºC/gas 4 and roast for two hours. Finish off with a hot blast at 200ºC/gas 5 for another 30 minutes.

Heat some olive oil and fry the bacon strips until golden, add the shredded savoy cabbage and cook until soft. Pour on the double cream, bring to the boil and reduce until it reaches a thick sauce consistency. Season.

Core and cut each apple into six wedges, heat the butter in a pan and cook them for one to two minutes. Then add the sugar and balsamic vinegar and reduce until the apple wedges are nice glazed.

Cut the pork back fat rind into long thin strips, lay on a baking tray, drizzle with olive oil and season before cooking in a pre-heated oven until a crispy crackling is achieved.

Place the creamed cabbage into the centre of the plate, top with pork belly and crackling and spoon apple wedges and jus around. Serve with crackling strips resting on the pork belly.

140g CHOPPED DARK CHOCOLATE
70 PER CENT COCOA CONTENT
225g BUTTER
5 EGGS
450g CASTER SUGAR
110g PLAIN FLOUR
55g COCOA POWDER

CHOCOLATE BROWNIE

Heat the oven to 190ºC/gas 5. Line a 20x30cm roasting tin with baking parchment. Gently melt the butter and the sugar together in a large pan. Take off the heat and beat in the rest of the ingredients.

Spoon the brownie batter into the prepared cake tin and shake gently until level. Transfer the tin to the oven and bake for 30-35 minutes, or until a skewer inserted into the centre of the brownies comes out clean. Set aside to cool. Take out of the oven and cool in the tin, then cut into 5cm squares.

BROWNS FRUITY MAI TAI

37.5ml Appleton's V/X
12.5ml Apricot Brandy
37.5ml orange juice
12.5ml pineapple juice
25ml orgeat syrup
Dash grenadine

Shake all ingredients, except grenadine, with cubed ice. Fill glass with crushed ice, strain into glass. Add dash of grenadine. Garnish with an orange slice.

APPLETON ESTATE
—SINCE 1749—
JAMAICA RUM

This toothsome mix of rum and tropical fruit juices has a Polynesian image. Yet the original Mai Tai appeared in its classic form at Trader Vic's restaurant in Oakland, California in 1944.

The Trader (Victor J Bergeron) created it one afternoon for some friends who were visiting from Tahiti. One of those friends, Carrie Guild, tasted it and cried out..

"MAITA'I ROA AE!"

(Literally in the Tahitian language "Very Good!", figuratively "Out of this world!")

It never shook off that South Seas glamour, featuring prominently in the Elvis Presley film, Blue Hawaii, and fuelling the rise of tiki bars. Our Browns version includes apricot brandy for that extra fruitiness.

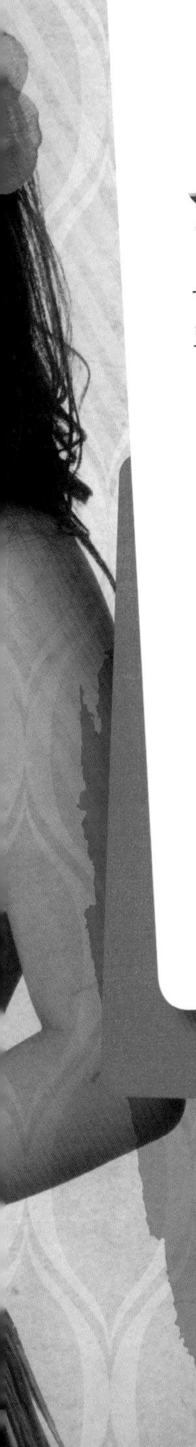

http://www.

Search

MUSICAL accompaniment

PRINCE AND THE NEW POWER GENERATION Diamonds and Pearls
PRIMAL SCREAM Screamadelica THE COMMITMENTS Soundtrack QUEEN
Innuendo REM Out of Time

JANET JACKSON signs a $30 million (US) record contract, which makes her the highest paid female recording artist ever

Hello World

Pixie Lott
Ed Sheeran
Diana Vickers
Jedward
Joe McElderry

sporting LIFE

MIKE TYSON wins his first world boxing title in Las Vegas. Scottish runner LIZ McCOLGAN becomes the first British gold medallist at the World Athletics Championships in Tokyo. At Wimbledon, MICHAEL STICH and STEFFI GRAF are champions.

IN THE NEWS...

The final breakthrough in the CHANNEL TUNNEL is achieved when the last section of clay in the South rail tunnel is bored away. The GULF WAR BEGINS, as the Royal Air Force joins Allied aircraft in bombing raids on Iraq. STELLA RIMINGTON becomes the first female head of MI5. TERRY WAITE is freed after four-and-a-half years in captivity.

The Soviet Union is formally dissolved.

DEBUTS on the box...

Mr Bean, Bottom, Noel's House Party Prime Suspect, SOLDIER SOLDIER

1991

Browns RESTAURANT & BAR

BEAUTIFUL BUILDINGS AND BROWNS GO TOGETHER and they certainly strike gold with Bristol where they convert a former museum modelled on The Doge's Palace in Venice.

FLORAL BABYDOLL DRESSES AND BIG BOOTS WERE

FASHION statements

and for him there were puffa jackets and James Happy Flower t-shirts [for girls as well]

HOOK, ROBIN HOOD PRINCE OF THIEVES, THE ADDAMS FAMILY, The Silence of the Lambs, Hot Shots! were all on the...

SILVER SCREEN

MOULES marinières

3,500g cooked mussels in full shell
25g prepared garlic
60ml cream and white wine sauce
10g flat leaf parsley
100g diced onions
20ml white wine
250ml double cream
100g unsalted butter

Bread & Butter PUDDING

50g UNSALTED BUTTER
250ml MILK
150ml COCONUT MILK/CREAM
2tbsp SUGAR
2 EGGS
50g SULTANAS
10 slices WHITE BREAD
50g DESICCATED COCONUT
1tsp VANILLA EXTRACT
4 CARDAMOM PODS

Chop the garlic and parsley. In a hot, oiled pan sweat off the onions and garlic, avoiding colouring them. Add the wine to the pan and reduce by half, then include the cream.

Bring the cream and white wine sauce to the boil and add mussels. Cooking should take five minutes and the mussels should all open. Any that don't, discard.

Place in the mussel pot and sprinkle on the parsley.

Accompany with fries and wholemeal bread.

Heat oven to 180ºC/gas 4. Grease your dish. Remove crusts from bread slices and cut in half diagonally, so they are triangles. Butter on one side of each.

Place half the slices of bread in your dish, butter side up, making sure the dish is covered. Sprinkle half the sultanas over the bread slices. Add the other half of the bread to make another layer and sprinkle on the remaining sultanas. Gently heat together the milk, cardamom, coconut cream and desiccated coconut. Once it starts to boil, remove from heat and let it rest while you do the next step.

Beat eggs, three quarters of the sugar and vanilla extract with an electric whisk until fluffy and pale (about three to five minutes) You need lots of air and bubbles!

Very carefully pour the whisked eggs into the coconut milk mixture. Once you have layered the bread and dried fruit to three quarters way up the bowl, pour over the liquid mixture, then continue layering bread to the top of the bowl. Cook for 20-25 minutes at 200ºC/gas 5.

Calves' Liver with Black Pudding

serves 4

4 220g slices calves' liver
8 slices pancetta (2 each)
4 50g slices black pudding
300g red wine jus

BUBBLE AND SQUEAK ACCOMPANIMENT

600g mashed potato
90ml virgin olive oil
225g savoy cabbage
60g peeled shallots
4 lemon wedges, 1 each
70g spring onions
10g chives, finely chopped

Prepare the bubble and squeak in advance. Shred the savoy cabbage and blanch in boiling salted water. Finely slice the shallots and spring onions and saute in a hot pan with a little oil.

Mix the mash with the cabbage, spring onions and shallots. Season and fold in the chopped chives. Portion into 150g chunks and form into oval shaped cakes. Make the jus by reducing red wine down and adding stock.

Now dust the calves' liver in the flour and place into a hot oiled pan. Cook until golden brown, turn and repeat, remove from the heat and rest for a minimum of two minutes.

Pan fry the bubble and squeak portion in a little butter until golden brown. Grill the pancetta and black pudding on a tray until golden and crispy.

Plate the heated bubble and squeak, top with the black pudding, calves' liver and pancetta, pour the red wine jus around and serve.

LONG JERRY ICED TEA

SAILOR JERRY®

12.5ml SAILOR JERRY
25ml CHERRY VODKA
12.5ml FINLANDIA LIME VODKA
Dash gomme syrup
Squeeze lemon
12.5ml sugar syrup
25ml lemon juice
PEPSI

SHAKE ingredients with cubed ice.
STRAIN over cubed ice, top with Pepsi.
GARNISH with maraschino cherry
and lemon wheel.

‹ 50 ›

This is our special pepped up twist on Long Island Iced Tea.

Sailor Jerry teams up with cherry and lime vodkas. This heady highball mix is tempered by a top-up of Pepsi.

There are too many claimants for the invention of Iced Teas – several from Long Island, naturally, but also other corners of the States.

Its innocent tea-like look helped it during Prohibition in the Twenties when the illegal consumption of alcohol was kept very low-key.

FASHION
STATEMENTS

for her were fitted jackets, short skirts and high heels. Teens wore slip dresses with tiny T-shirts or mini-kilts with skinny-ribbed tops with Mary Janes and thigh-highs.

For him, the relaxed look was replaced with a sharply tailored appearance, and Jean Paul Gaultier advocated the kilt...

"GLAMOUR" REPLACED "CASUAL CHIC"

1994

BROWNS PREPARES TO CONQUER LONDON

by acquiring a small bar in Draycott Avenue, Chelsea. This is to prove too small but it paves the way for glamorous Mayfair and Covent Garden, still with us today.

BRAZIL WINS THE FIFA WORLD CUP

Forty-five-year-old **GEORGE FOREMAN** wins in Las Vegas and becomes boxing's oldest heavyweight champion. **MICHAEL SCHUMACHER** wins the Formula One Drivers' Championship. At Wimbledon, **PETE SAMPRAS** and **CONCHITA MARTÍNEZ** are champions.

HELLO WORLD

HARRY STYLES of One Direction, British diver **TOM DALEY,** Irish actress **SAOIRSE RONAN** and Paralympic swimmer **ELLIE SIMMONS**

SPORTING LIFE

REDNEX, MARIAH CAREY were in the singles charts – and of course WET WET WET remains at no 1 for 15 weeks with 'Love is All Around'

MUSICAL ACCOMPANIMENT

TORI AMOS Under the Pink
MORRISSEY Vauxhall and I
OASIS Definitely Maybe
M PEOPLE Bizarre Fruit
BLUR Parklife

IN THE NEWS

The first **FEMALE PRIESTS** are ordained by The Church of England

The **CHANNEL TUNNEL**, which took over 7 years to complete, opens the UK's land link to France & Europe

Following the first democratic election, the Republic of **SOUTH AFRICA REJOINS THE BRITISH COMMONWEALTH**

BBC1 airs the first **NATIONAL LOTTERY** draw, hosted by Noel Edmonds

The Mask, Four Weddings and a Funeral, The Lion King, Forrest Gump and The Flintstones were all on the...

SILVER SCREEN

DEBUTS ON THE BOX...

The Vicar of Dibley, The Fast Show, **READY STEADY COOK**, Wycliffe, Time Team

1994

8 100g pieces of monkfish, 2 each
15g unsalted butter
Half a savoy cabbage, shredded
4 slices of smoked streaky bacon
100ml double cream
20ml olive oil
2 lemons, halved

CRAB&PRAWN
linguine

SERVES

4

400g linguine
32 king prawns (8 each)
100g crab meat
150g lime and chilli pesto
Drizzle olive oil
4 lime halves, 1 each

LIME & CHILLI PESTO
(makes 500g)

4 limes, juice and zest
500ml olive oil
20g red chillies, finely chopped
200g grated Parmesan
40g peeled garlic cloves
60g chopped coriander leaves

Slice the prawns down the back to form a butterfly. Prepare the lime and chilli pesto by zesting and squeezing the limes. Blitz the juice and zest with all the other ingredients with a hand blender. It makes much more than you need but it's easier to process in these quantities and keeps well in a jar in the fridge.

Cook the pasta until al dente in boiling, seasoned water. In a hot, oiled pan place the butterflied prawns, saute for 2-3 minutes. Add the prepared linguine to the pan and mix together. Add crab meat and pesto. Chargrill the lime half. Place in warmed small pasta bowls and garnish with pea shoots, lime half and herbs or micro salad of your choice.

MONKFISH
with creamed cabbage

Cut the streaky bacon into strips. Shred the cabbage.

Fry the bacon strips in olive oil until golden, add the shredded cabbage and cook until soft. Pour on the double cream, bring to the boil and reduce until it reaches a thick sauce consistency. Season.

Melt the butter in a hot pan and cook the monkfish on all sides until lightly coloured. Transfer briefly to a warm oven to finish cooking.

Reheat the creamed cabbage and place it in the centre of each plate, topped with monkfish. Serve with a lemon half and a suggested accompaniment of potato rosti.

SALTED CARAMEL
cheesecake

Mix the melted butter with the crushed breadcrumbs and press into a flan ring. Boil the double cream in a pan, add the chocolate and stir until melted. Remove from the heat and cool. Beat together the cream cheese, sugar, maple syrup and eggs, then add the cream and chocolate mix. Pour over the biscuit base and cook in a preheated oven 165ºC/gas 3 for approximately 20 minutes. Remove from the oven and cool.

Place the caster sugar in a pan with 2 tbsp of water and bring to the boil. Continue cooking until a light golden brown. Add the condensed milk and sea salt and stir until dissolved. Cool. Serve a slice of the cheesecake with the sauce drizzled over.

BISCUIT BASE
150g melted butter
350g crushed digestives

CHEESECAKE MIX
750g cream cheese
75g dark brown sugar
100ml double cream
100g bitter chocolate
25ml maple syrup
3 eggs

SALTED CARAMEL SAUCE
75g caster sugar
25g butter
75ml condensed milk
5g flaked sea salt

RÉMY MARTIN
FINE CHAMPAGNE COGNAC

125ml Mercier Champagne
12.5ml Remy Martin
Single sugar cube
4 dashes angostura bitters

Soak sugar cube in bitters.
Pour brandy in, followed by champagne.
Drop in the sugar cube.

CHAMPAGNE COCKTAIL

From Bellinis to Buck's Fizz, bubbly's a brilliant base for a sparkling cocktail, whether you simply add floral fruit syrups or hard liquor.

Browns' version packs a punch by combining smooth, aromatic Remy Martin brandy, all cloves and vanilla, with Mercier, a classic champagne blend with a nose of pears and fresh bread, then a long, fresh taste.

The herbiness of the bitters acts as ringmaster to this classy combo.

in the
NEWS

1997

British Scientists announce that a sheep named Dolly had been successfully cloned, and was born in July 1996. Tony Blair becomes Prime Minister. J. K. Rowling's Harry Potter and the Philosopher's Stone is published. The United Kingdom hands sovereignty of Hong Kong to the People's Republic of China. A TV audience of over 2 billion watches the funeral of Diana, Princess of Wales, at Westminster Abbey.

BROWNS™
RESTAURANT & BAR

Browns gets ready for major change as Bass prepares to take over the business in 1998 – and over the following years open eight new branches.

SPORTING
life

HELLO
world!

DYLAN JAGGER is born to Pamela Anderson and Tommy Lee, **GABRIEL LUKE BEAUREGARD** to Jerry Hall and Mick Jagger, **AVA ELIZABETH** to Heather Locklear and Richie Sambora and **SIAN BEATRICE ECHO** to proud parents The Edge and Morleigh Steinberg.

Tiger Woods becomes the first African-American to win the US Masters Golf Tournament. Jacques Villeneuve of Canada wins the Formula One Championship. At Wimbledon, Pete Sampras and Martina Hingis are champions.

FASHION
statements

...for her, Cool Britannia and Spice Girls influences with Union Jack motifs on dresses and tops...also, tight miniskirts and low waisted flared jeans. Single breasted suits and jackets were big for him. Chelsea boots, designer branded polo shirts, and jeans teamed with skater shoes.

MUSICAL
accompaniment

PAUL WELLER Heavy Soul
OASIS Be Here Now
ROBBIE WILLIAMS Life thru a Lens
SPICE GIRLS Spice World
THE VERVE Urban Hymns
BLUR Blur

Be Here Now
Oasis's third album, becomes the fastest selling album in UK history

DEBUTS
on the box...

Teletubbies, Jonathan Creek, I'm Alan Partridge, Midsomer Murders, Where The Heart Is and Brass Eye.

Katrina and the Waves win the Eurovision Song Contest for the UK

Hanson, Aqua, No Doubt, Steps and Cornershop were in the singles charts

Titanic, Men In Black, **L.A. Confidential**, The Full Monty, **Con Air**, Tomorrow Never Dies were all on the...

Silver Screen

Lobster & Scallop
THERMIDOR

2 lobsters, halved
250g king scallops
600g cherry tomatoes on the vine
60ml olive oil
100g spinach

THERMIDOR SAUCE

120g shallots, finely chopped
160ml white wine
100g English mustard
40ml water
300ml double cream
40g Cheddar cheese
Handful chopped tarragon
1 egg yolk

Coat the tomatoes in the oil and roast in a hot oven. To make the Thermidor sauce, place the finely chopped shallots, white wine and mustard in a pan, bring to the boil and reduce until all the liquid has evaporated.

Add the water and double cream, bring to the boil and reduce by half. Remove from the heat and beat in the cheese and chopped tarragon. Do not reboil. Chill in a fridge and beat in the egg yolk. For the lobster, remove the meat from the shell and dice into chunks.

Halve the scallops and place in a bowl with the lobster pieces. Coat with the sauce and return back to the shell.

Serve, accompanied by rocket and parmesan salad.

OYSTERS
with Tabasco

24 oysters (6 each)
2 lemons halved
8 tbsp red wine vinegar and finely chopped shallot dressing
Handful of dried seaweed

Open the oysters, serve on crushed ice with seaweed and lemon as garnish with the dressing and perhaps Tabasco on the side.

500ml double cream
1 vanilla pod
100g caster sugar (plus extra for the topping)
6 free-range egg yolks

Creme Brulee

Preheat the oven to 150ºC/gas 2. Pour the cream into a saucepan. Split the vanilla pod lengthways and scrape the seeds into the cream. Chop the empty pod into small pieces, and add them to the cream. Bring the cream to boiling point, then reduce the heat and simmer gently for five minutes. Meanwhile, in a separate bowl, beat the sugar and egg yolks together in a large heatproof bowl until pale and fluffy. Bring the cream back to boiling point. Pour it over the egg mixture, whisking continuously until thickened – this indicates that the eggs have begun to cook slightly.

Strain the mixture through a fine sieve into a large jug, and then use this to fill six ramekins to about two-thirds full. Place the ramekins into a large roasting tray and pour in enough hot water to come half way up their outsides. This is a form of bain-marie. Place the bain-marie on the centre shelf of the oven and bake for 40-45 minutes, or until the custards are just set but wobbly in the middle. Remove the ramekins from the water and set aside to cool to room temperature. When ready to serve, sprinkle one level teaspoon of caster sugar evenly over the surface of each creme brulee, then caramelise with a chefs' blow-torch, if you have one. Otherwise flash under the grill.

37.5ml Finlandia Grapefruit Vodka
12.5ml Cointreau
12.5ml lemon juice
25ml cranberry juice

SHAKE all ingredients with cubed ice.
DOUBLE strain into a glass.
GARNISH with orange peel.

GRAPEFRUIT
Cosmopolitan

We think you'll find our own, zingy citrus version as sexy as, well, Sex In The City, the late 1990s telly smash that really put this Seventies stalwart firmly back on the map.

Cosmos were what Sarah Jessica Parker's character, Carrie Bradshaw, invariably ordered when out with the girls around New York.

The cocktail, a cousin of cranberry coolers, has maintained its phenomenal popularity despite Carrie explaining in the film adaptation why she had stopped drinking them: **"Because everyone else started."**

Fickle girl. She'd still be hooked if she'd ever encountered Browns' grapefruit version, mingling Finlandia's grapefruit-infused vodka kick with the warm orange glow from the Cointreau!

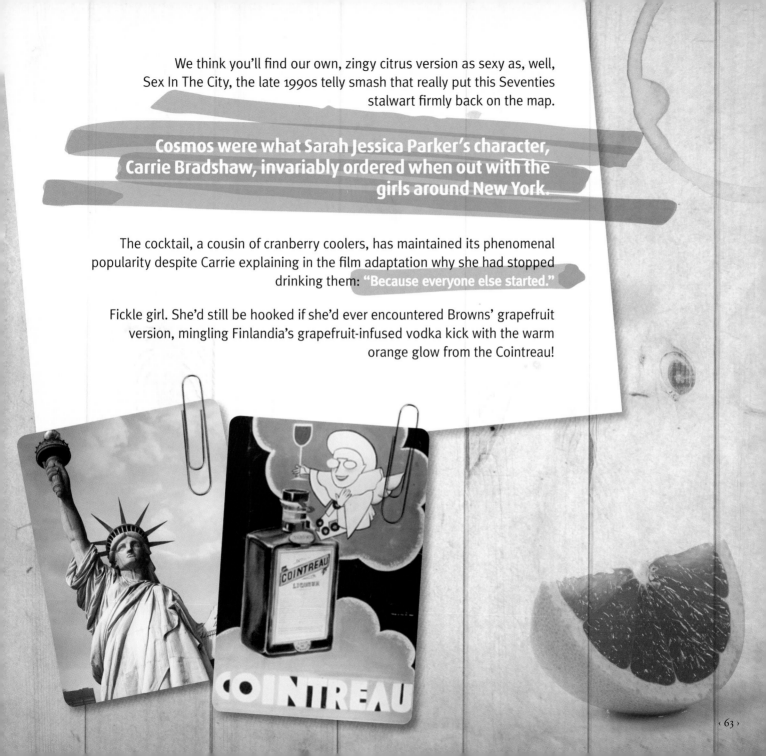

COINTREAU

00s

the OUGHTIES

Hello world

ELLA CORINNE was born to Annette Bening and Warren Beatty, LEO GEORGE to Tony Blair and Cherie Blair, ALEXANDRIA ZAHRA to David Bowie and Iman Bowie, ROCCO JOHN to Guy Ritchie and Madonna, JERMAJESTY to Jermaine Jackson and Alejandra Genevieve Oiaza and ELLA BLEU was born to proud parents John Travolta and Kelly Preston

THE PERFECT STORM, GLADIATOR, CAST AWAY, X-Men and What Lies Beneath were on the

SILVER SCREEN

Sporting LIFE

GREAT BRITAIN COMPETES AT THE OLYMPICS IN SYDNEY AND WINS 11 GOLD, 10 SILVER AND 7 BRONZE MEDALS. The 77-year-old Wembley Stadium closes, to be re-built and re-opened in 2007. At Wimbledon, Pete Sampras and Venus Williams are champions.

Notable Album Releases

ANASTACIA Not That Kind

BRITNEY SPEARS Oops! I Did It Again

EMINEM The Marshall Mathers LP

COLDPLAY Parachutes

MADONNA Music

Monarch Of The Glen, Doctors, BIG BROTHER and The Wright Stuff were...

debut on the box...

In The News...

The 21st century begins with celebrations all over the world. Vladimir Putin is elected President of Russia. The Tate Modern Gallery opens in London. After 41 years, the last Mini is produced in Longbridge.

QUEEN ELIZABETH THE QUEEN MOTHER CELEBRATES HER 100TH BIRTHDAY

2000

BROWNS™
RESTAURANT & BAR

LONDON CALLING!
Browns opens in West India Quay, to be swiftly followed by Old Jewry, Islington, Windsor and Butler's Wharf on the Thames with its spectacular view of Tower Bridge.

FASHION statements

for her were denim jackets, print skirts with designer bags and flash jewellery. For him, cargo pants with zip-off legs, Adidas or Nike trainers, lumberjack shirts, Puffer or Berghaus jackets were all the rage.

GHETTO *Fabulous*

Roasted Goat's Cheese

40g raspberry vinaigrette *(recipe opposite)*
100g dried cherry tomatoes *(recipe opposite)*
4 baby goat's cheeses
40g panko breadcrumbs
handful sliced radishes
20g walnut halves
20ml olive oil
4 crostini sticks
40g rocket

Mix together all the ingredients to make raspberry vinaigrette.

Likewise for the mango & chilli salsa and leave to stand for a few minutes, or for up to three hours in the fridge.

Slice the cherry tomatoes in half, then place on a baking sheet. Drizzle with oil and sprinkle with garlic and rosemary. Dry in a low oven for up to two hours until softened but still intact while also being caramelised. To compose the salad, place the walnut halves and panko breadcrumbs in a bowl, crush together, ensuring they're well mixed. Place each baby goat's cheese into the mix and coat all over, pressing down to encrust each cheese, then lay on a tray.

Place the goats cheese under a grill, until golden brown, turn and repeat on other side of cheese. Dress the rocket, cherry tomatoes and radish in a bowl with a spoonful of raspberry vinaigrette. Toss together and place a portion on each plate. Spoon the mango salsa on and top with goat's cheese. Drizzle with remaining raspberry vinaigrette. Accompany with a spicy relish or salsa of your choice.

RASPBERRY VINAIGRETTE
(makes 650ml)
300g raspberries in sugar sauce
200ml olive oil
150ml white wine vinegar

DRIED TOMATOES
1 punnet cherry tomatoes
10g diced garlic
5g finely chopped rosemary

MANGO AND CHILLI SALSA
1 mango, peeled and diced
Half a small red onion, finely chopped
Half a red chilli, finely chopped
Juice of a lime

DUCK LEG
Cassoulet

4 confit duck legs, 1 each
1kg pork belly
120g haricot beans
120g garlic sausage
50g streaky bacon, finely diced
140g diced carrots
140g diced celery
120g diced onions
2 cloves peeled garlic
250g cooked cannellini beans
180g plum tomatoes, chopped
20g herbed breadcrumbs
25g red wine jus
Fresh herbs, a bay leaf and water to top up

4 servings

Make the jus by reducing down red wine and adding stock. To prepare the duck confit, first ask your butcher to cut the knuckles off the four duck legs. In a hot pan heat some oil and colour the legs on both sides until golden brown. Place them in a tray and cover with duck fat, then put a preheated oven at 120C for 2.5-3 hours or until tender.

Sprinkle with breadcrumbs and gratinate under an overhead grill. To make cassoulet base, heat some oil in a large pan and fry the bacon until golden. Add the onions, carrots, celery with garlic sausage and cook until softened. Do not allow to colour too much. Mix in cannellini beans, tomatoes, bay leaf and appropriate herbs such as parsley and thyme plus salt and pepper and cook for a few minutes more. If too dry, add extra water.

Plate each portion of cassoulet topped with a duck leg and drizzle hot wine jus around. French beans are the recommended accompaniment.

Afternoon Tea

At Browns it comes with an added, zesty twist – turn overleaf...

‹ 69 ›

Elderflower & Cucumber Collins

"Tom Collins" was the focus of a US-wide hoax in 1874.

"Have you seen Tom Collins?"

...a listener was asked. When he replied he didn't know anyone of that name, he was told TC was around the corner in a bar, talking about the listener to others. It inevitably sparked a kerfuffle.

OK, pre-movies and TV people had to make their own amusement! Whatever, within two years the hoax was celebrated in a cocktail of that name, often shortened to Collins.

That was basically gin and lemon.

Much more sophisticated – and refreshing – is Browns' current take on the drink, where elderflower cordial and diced cucumber are a perfect springlike match for newly released cult gin Hendrick's (which actually uses cucumber – and rose petals – among its infusions).

50ml Hendrick's Gin
20ml elderflower cordial
12.5ml lemon juice
Handful cucumber slices

Muddle cucumber in a glass, add all your other ingredients plus cubed ice and shake. Strain over cubed ice into a glass and garnish with more cucumber.

A most unusual Afternoon Tea...

All that summer greenery must be good for you!

Browns serve an exquisite range of teas to accompany our duo of classic sandwiches – salmon and cucumber, each teamed with cream cheese in a fresh-tasting filling. The bread, of course, has to be sliced white, crustless and slightly sticky.

For a special twist treat yourself to an Elderflower and Cucumber Collins, too.

RHIANNA A Girl Like Me
SNOW PATROL Eyes Open
TAKE THAT Beautiful World

Notable Album Releases

GOSSIP Standing In The Way Of Control
KT TUNSTALL Eye To The Telescope
NE-YO In My Own Words

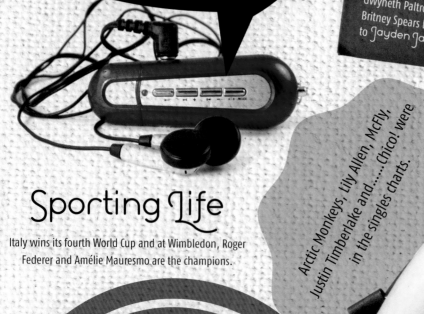

Hello World!

Suri was born to Tom Cruise and Katie Holmes, Shiloh Nouvel Jolie-Pitt to Brad Pitt and Angelina Jolie, Moses to Chris Martin and Gwyneth Paltrow and, Kevin Federline and Britney Spears became proud parents to Jayden James Federline.

Sporting Life

Italy wins its fourth World Cup and at Wimbledon, Roger Federer and Amélie Mauresmo are the champions.

Arctic Monkeys, Lily Allen, McFly, Justin Timberlake and......Chico! were in the singles charts.

In The News

Her Majesty Elizabeth II celebrates her 80th birthday. The Anglo-American loan made in 1946 is paid off by The British Government. The one billionth song is bought from iTunes. The UK and Europe has a July heatwave. Google buys YouTube.

2006

BIG PLAYERS!
Browns owners Mitchells & Butlers, once the pub division of Bass, are now the leading restaurant and pub company in the UK.

The Da Vinci Code, Casino Royale, Night At The Museum, Happy Feet, The Devil Wears Prada, King Kong were all on the...

Silver Screen

Debuts on the box ...

Life On Mars, Hotel Babylon, Waterloo Road, Dancing On Ice, The IT Crowd, Torchwood were...

Fashion statements
...for her were shorts or minis with opaque tights, skinny jeans, OVERSIZED SUNGLASSES and BIG DESIGNER BAGS. For him, there were peacoats, slim-cut shirts, converse and slouchy beanie hats.

73

Dinner Party Favourites

360g salmon fillet
120g Pico de Gallo salsa (recipe below)
60g cucumber
80g peeled carrots
80ml orange, lemon and piquillo pepper vinaigrette

Vinaigrette

2 medium oranges
2 lemons
30g whole piquillo pepper
150m virgin olive oil

Pico de Gallo

4 ripe large tomatoes, seeded and chopped
Handful fresh coriander, washed and chopped
2 garlic cloves, peeled and finely chopped
1 small red onion, finely chopped
1 tbsp fresh lime juice
1 clove garlic
1 pinch cumin
Salt and pepper

Minute of Salmon

To make the vinaigrette, chop pequillo peppers finely, removing any seeds. Squeeze the juice from the oranges and lemons and pass through a fine sieve. Whisk together citrus juice, peppers and olive oil and season. For Pico de Gallo, stir the tomatoes, onion, coriander, jalapeno pepper, lime juice, garlic, garlic, cumin, salt, and pepper together in a bowl. Refrigerate at least three hours before serving.

Remove pin bones from salmon fillet and slice it into thin slices, 2mm thick. Cut the carrot and cucumber into matchsticks (with the latter, discarding the seeds). Lay the sliced salmon portion in a neat circle on a large square plate, ensuring the salmon does not overlap and is only a single layer thick. Drizzle the vinaigrette over the salmon, ensuring complete coverage and season with sea salt and cracked black pepper. Grill for 3-4 minutes until cooked, but still slightly pink in the middle. Spoon the Pico de Gallo salsa (or your favourite relish) over the centre of the salmon.

Red wine and Vanilla Poached Pear with Figs

Seabass with Curry

8 seabass fillets, 2 each
4 sweet potatoes
200g baby spinach
200g boiled chickpeas
small bunch mint and parsley

Yoghurt and caper dressing

300g Greek yoghurt
60g chopped capers
Dessert spoon chopped chives
1 lime, juice and zest

Curry sauce

250g onions, finely chopped
3 cloves garlic, finely chopped
10ml olive oil
0g chopped tinned tomatoes
10g Madras curry powder
120ml water
Salt and pepper

4 peeled and cored pears
2 fresh figs (half each)
Half bottle bottle red wine
100ml frozen honey yoghurt
1 vanilla pod
20ml balsamic vinegar
115g sugar
10g demerara sugar

To make the curry sauce, in a large saucepan saute the onions and garlic in oil until lightly coloured, add the curry powder and cook for 2-3 minutes, add the tomatoes and water, stir well, bring to the boil and simmer for 20-25 minutes. Season. Liquidise the sauce until smooth.

Prepare the yoghurt and caper dressing by mixing all the ingredients together. Roast the diced sweet potato in the oven until golden brown. MIx the roasted sweet potato, baby spinach, curry sauce, chick peas, chopped herbs and olive oil. Season and oil the seabass fillets, then place on a tray under a grill, skin side up, and cook until the skin starts to colour.

Spoon a portion of sweet potato, spinach and curry mix in the the centre of each plate, placing sea bass fillets on top of each. Serve garnished with the caper and yoghurt dressing with naan or any flatbread of your choice.

Put pears in a large pan with wine, vanilla, balsamic and both sugars and cook gently for 20 to 30 minutes. Add figs towards the end to soften but not mushy. Take out pears and figs and build on a plate with yoghurt. Drizzle pan juice over and garnish with a sprig of mint, if you wish.

African Gin Sling

Recreations of the famous Singapore Sling can often be a pre-mixed shadow of the original. Better to go African in Browns with our truly innovative Sling.

5ml Whitley Neill Gin
25ml Tia Maria
50ml Cracker Mango &
Passion Fruit Juice
25ml lemon juice
12.5ml sugar syrup
Dash Angostura Bitters

Shake all ingredients with cubed ice in a glass, top with soda. Garnish with a lemon wheel.

Another beautifully accomplished gin goes into the African Sling, along with Tia Maria and some vivid, exotic juices.

This time it's Whitley Neill, a new premium London Dry Gin steeped with coriander and juniper prior to distillation in antique copper pot stills. Its "African" flavour comes from two signature botanicals from that continent – the Cape Gooseberry and the fruit of the Baobob tree.

Slings in America were originally gin with sweetened, flavoured water. It took a bartender at Raffles Hotel, Singapore to transform them with the addition of cherry brandy and fresh tropical juices.

Vintage & Retro chic...

were fashion statements for her – pre-worn dresses and accessories. For him, jumpers, deep v neck cardigans, collarless leather jackets and distressed leather boots were popular.

2009

In The News

Swine Flu becomes a global pandemic. **Michael Jackson** dies triggering worldwide grief. After 100 years, **Woolworths** close all their stores. **Slumdog Millionaire** sweeps the board with four Golden Globes, seven BAFTA's and eight Oscars. **Sir Terry Wogan** presents his final breakfast show on BBC Radio 2 After 27 years. In December, **heavy snowfall** causes widespread disruption across large parts of the UK

Silver screen

hits included ANGELS & DEMONS, THE HANGOVER, SHERLOCK HOLMES, 2012 and Avatar

Sporting Life

England wins The Ashes. Jenson Button wins the F1 World Championship. At Wimbledon, Roger Federer and Serena Williams are champions

Notable Album Releases

SUSAN BOYLE – I Dreamed A Dream
BLACK EYED PEAS – The E.N.D.
MICHAEL JACKSON – This Is It
MICHAEL BUBLE – Crazy Love
LADY GAGA – The Fame

Debuts on the box...

were Total Wipeout, Being Human, WHITECHAPEL, Piers Morgan's Life Stories and Law & Order UK

Hello World!

Lou Sulola is born to Heidi Klum and Seal, Twin girls Marion Loretta Elwell and Tabitha Hodge to Sarah Jessica Parker and Matthew Broderick, Harper Willow to Dave Grohl and Jordyn Blum, and Melanie Chisholm and Thomas Starr become proud parents to Scarlett

Alexandra Burke, Lilly Allen, Calvin Harris-, Pixie Lott, La Roux and Cheryl Cole were in the singles charts

‹ 79 ›

Chicory, Roquefort & Hazelnut Salad

120g red chicory
120g white chicory
40g rocket
1 cos lettuce
60g red onion
2 Braeburn apples
80g peeled hazelnuts
240g Roquefort cheese
10g chopped chives

vinaigrette

80ml olive oil
40ml sherry vinegar

Prepare the sherry vinaigrette by mixing the oil and vinegar (red or white can substitute). Trim the red and white chicory and cos lettuce. Finely slice the red onions.

Roast the hazelnuts in the oven, remove from the oven and crush (not too finely), ensuring some large pieces remain, cool.

Crumble 120g of the Roquefort and mix with chicory, rocket, cos, apples, red onions and chives in a bowl and dress gently with the sherry vinaigrette.

Arrange down the centre of a rectangular plate and sprinkle with the chopped hazelnuts and remaining Roquefort.

Drizzle a little vinaigrette around and serve.

Haunch of Venison

Trio of Chocolate Brownies

Heat the oven to 190°c/gas 5. Line a 20 x 30cm roasting tin with baking parchment.

For the first two brownies gently melt the butter and the sugar together in a large pan. Take off the heat and beat in the rest of the ingredients. Spoon the brownie batter into the prepared cake tin and shake gently until level. Transfer the tin to the oven and bake for 30-35 minutes, or until a skewer inserted into the centre of the brownies comes out clean. Set aside to cool. Take out of the oven and cool in the tin, then cut into 5cm squares.

Dark

140g chopped dark chocolate (70 per cent cocoa content)

225g butter

5 eggs

450g caster sugar

110g plain flour

55g cocoa powder

Milk & Ginger

140g milk chocolate

225g butter

5 eggs

450g caster sugar

110g plain flour

55g drinking chocolate

2tsp of ground ginger

Blondie

225g caster sugar

4 free-range eggs

225g butter, melted, plus extra for greasing

150g plain flour, sifted

225g white chocolate, chopped

100g raspberries

2tsp of ground ginger

Beat together the sugar and eggs until pale and fluffy. Beat in the melted butter a little at a time, making sure each addition of butter is fully incorporated before adding the next. Add the flour and carefully fold it into the mixture, using a metal spoon. Carefully fold the white chocolate and raspberries into the mixture, ensuring the raspberries do not break up.

Spoon the brownie batter into the prepared cake tin and shake gently until level. Transfer the tin to the oven and bake for 30-35 minutes, or until a skewer inserted into the centre comes out clean. Set aside to cool. Serve in 5cm slices.

reaks of venison haunch
1 x 150g)
celeriac
edcurrant reduction

the celeriac two ways. First peel, putting the riac into water with lemon juice to prevent it wning. Then slice a quarter of it very finely, t in flour and deep fry to make crisps.

the remaining three quarters for around minutes until soft and then puree in a der with milk, butter and salt and pepper.

e the redcurrant reduction by reducing ml of red wine and mixing in 4tbsp of currant jelly.

fry the venison steaks swiftly. A couple ninutes will do, keeping them pink. erwise they get tough. Serve with the riac and a drizzle of the warm redcurrant uction. A sweet potato dauphinoise makes vely accompaniment.

BACARDI

ESTD CUBA 1862

50ml Bacardi Superior
75ml champagne
12.5ml gomme syrup
8 mint leaves
8 lime wedges

Muddle lime wedges and mint,
add Bacardi, gomme and crushed ice.
Mix well, then add more crushed
ice and top with champagne.
Garnish with mint.

Luxury Mojito

Luxury? Definitely.

Boosting the traditional mint, lime and rum rush with the fizz of good champagne
was a wizard idea. We're sure even the ubiquitous Ernest Hemingway would have approved. He was a huge
mojito fan and his hand-written tribute can still be read on the wall of his favourite Havana bar:

"My mojito in La Bodeguita, my daiquiri in El Floridiata"

The bubbly replaces the less charismatic soda, but the principles of a good mojito
are all followed in this luxury version.

Lime juice is added to or syrup and mint leaves. The mixture
is then gently mashed with a muddler (a bartender's
mashing tool). The mint leaves should only be bruised
to release the essential oils and should not be
shredded. Then rum is added and the mixture is briefly
stirred to integrate the syrup and lift the mint
leaves up from the bottom for better presentation.
The result is very moreish.

As they say in Cuba

Salud!

2013
DINNER PARTY FAVOURITES

RIBS

3 FULL RACKS OF PORK RIBS, CUT INTO 12 PIECES O

2-4 BONES EACH, TO SERVE THREE PER PERSON.

1 ONION,

2 BAYLEAVES

2 TSP PEPPERCORNS

UNREFINED RAW CANE SUGAR TO SPRINKLE

SAUCE

250ML ORANGE JUICE

250ML PINEAPPLE JUICE

60ML LEMON JUICE

60ML HONEY ¼ CUP

2 TBSP SOY SAUCE

3-4 GOOD SHAKES TABASCO

3-4 GOOD SHAKES WORCESTER SAUCE

220G UNREFINED RAW CANE SUGAR

120ML TOMATO KETCHUP

SIMMER THE RIBS in boiling water infused with onic
bay and peppercorns for 30 to 40 minutes.
Place ribs on a baking tray and sprinkle generously
with unrefined raw cane sugar and slowly roast at 12
- 140°C/gas 3 for 1 ½ hours. Baste with stock after 2
minutes and 40 minutes.
While the ribs are roasting, reduce the stock down
third of its original volume while skimming off any
top sediment. Remove the onions, bay and
peppercorns and add all remaining ingredients.
Stir well, then reduce down by simmering vigorousl
As it thickens and darkens baste the ribs one last tin
20 minutes before they are finished. Continue to
reduce the sauce until it is thick, sticky and dark.
Remove from the heat anf serve with a crisp baked
potato topped with sour cream with chopped fresh
chives, coleslaw and an fresh green salad.

SCALLOPS WITH CURRY

12 SCALLOPS, 3 EACH

4G CURRY POWDER

24 CAULIFLOWER FLORETS, 6 EACH

80G BOUGHT-IN TEMPURA BATTER

200G CAULIFLOWER PUREE

160G GRAPE VINAIGRETTE

GRAPE VINAIGRETTE

220G WHITE SEEDLESS GRAPES

20G PREPARED GARLIC

150G PEELED SHALLOTS

80ML WHITE WINE VINEGAR

200ML VIRGIN OLIVE OIL

PREPARE
THE GRAPE
vinaigrette by
cutting grapes into quarters
lengthways and chopping garlic
and shallots very finely. In a bowl whisk
together the white wine vinegar and olive oil and
add all the chopped mixture. Trim the cauliflower
into florets the size of a 1 pence piece, 24 in total,
then dust with curry powder. Dice the remainder
of the cauliflower, place in a pan and fully cover
with milk and simmer until very soft and cooked
through. Drain and liquidise, adding some milk if
necessary to achieve the correct consistency. Place
three pools of puree down the centre of each plate.
Dust the scallops on one side with curry powder
and place dusted side down in a very hot oiled pan
and cook for one minute on each side until dark
golden. Do not overcook. Season with sea salt
and place on top of the puree. Coat cauliflower
florets with tempura batter and deep fry until
golden brown. Add to plate and garnish with
grape vinaigrette.

8 4OZ BROWNS BURGER, 2 EACH	4 BEEF TOMATO SLICES
4 SEEDED BUNS	120G ONIONS
800G SKINNY FRIES	20G PLAIN FLOUR
4 MATURE CHEDDAR SLICES	20G TEMPURA BATTER
4 SLICES STREAKY BACON	120G APPLE AND CELERIAC SLAW
4 CUPS ICEBERG LETTUCE	120G RELISH OF YOUR CHOICE

CHUNKY KETCHUP, LIME & CHILLI MAYO, SLICED GHERKINS TO ACCOMPANY

·BROWNS· BURGER

BAR & BRASSERIE
·BROWNS·
ESTABLISHED 1973

FOLLOW MANUFACTURER'S INSTRUCTIONS for the tempura batter mix. Dip the onion rings into the plain flour and then into the tempura batter mix and cook until golden in the fryer. Tear off the iceberg lettuce leaves, keeping them intact to make iceberg cups, while discarding the core. Cut the tomatoes into 40g slices and the onions into very thin rings, then mix the apple and celeriac slaw with mayonnaise. To prepare the burgers, mince herbs, garlic, onions and 1,000g meat and form into eight burgers. Fry until crisp and deep brown on the outside, juicy and pink inside. Place the burgers on to the chargrill. Season while cooking on both sides. Sear until juices run clear. Cook the bacon on the chargrill until crisp.

While still on the grill, top the burgers with the bacon and then the cheese. Lightly toast the burger bun on the chargrill. Meanwhile, fry the chips. Remove, drain and season. Home-made skinny chips are easy to prepare and get to the perfect crisp texture. Cut the spuds into fine batons, drop them into a deep-fat frier (or deep pan) where garlic and herbs have been dropped in the oil.

CARPACCIO OF PINEAPPLE

500G PINEAPPLE
200G STRAWBERRIES
4 SCOOPS FROZEN YOGURT WITH HONEY
100ML LIME & CHILLI SYRUP

LIME & CHILLI SYRUP

1 LIME, ZEST AND JUICE
2G FINELY DICED CHILLIES
130G CASTER SUGAR
3G STAR ANISE
80ML WATER

To PREPARE lime and chilli syrup, finely grate the zest of the lime and sieve the juice. Place in a pan with remaining ingredients and bring to the boil.
Dice the strawberries, removing stalk, slice the pineapple very thinly (a mandolin is useful here), so it is flexible. Toss with a little of the lime and chilli syrup and fan across the plate.
Spoon over 25ml of syrup, ensuring to stir it first, garnish with honey cress and diced strawberries, then place a ball of the frozen honey yoghurt in centre of plate.

MACARONI CHEESE

450G UNCOOKED MACARONI

2TBSP CREME FRAICHE

60G CHIVES

250G DICED TALEGGIO CHEESE

250G MOZZARELLA PEARLS

120G GRATED GRUYERE

250G MASCARPONE

30G ENGLISH MUSTARD

40G PANKO BREADCRUMBS, TOASTED

40G SEMI-DRIED CHERRY TOMATOES

MIXED FRESH HERBS TO GARNISH

BOIL THE MACARONI until al dente and drain. Melt all the cheeses together with creme fraiche and chives, then add mustard. Mix in with the macaroni in a serving bowl. Top with breadcrumbs, bake in an oven at 160ºc/gas 3 for 20 minutes until bubbling and serve, accompanied by semi-dried cherry tomatoes and herbs.

FILO PARCEL WITH GOAT'S CHEESE, SWEET POTATO & PEA

16 FILO PASTRY SHEETS
(4 PLUS 2 EXTRA HELPINGS TO SHARE)

240G CRUSHED PEAS, SOFT NOT MUSH

240G SWEET POTATO PULP

SMALL TUB MASCARPONE CHEESE

400G GOAT'S CHEESE LOG

60G MELTED BUTTER

2 LARGE RED PEPPERS, ROASTED

60G WASHED ROCKET

PUT THE PEPPERS on a baking tray, drizzle with oil, season and then roast. Cut two sweet potatoes into, pieces and steam for 15 to 20 minutes, then mash. Dice the goat's cheese log, then mix together with the crushed peas, sweet potato pulp and mascarpone. Brush a sheet of filo with melted butter, fold the filo sheet in half and then half again to a create a square a quarter of the original size. Place a large spoonful of the prepared mix into the centre, crimp the filo together and twist to create a parcel. Brush the entire parcel with melted butter and place on a tray. Repeat until you have six, then place them in the oven at 160ºc/ gas 3 for up to 10 minutes until they are brown and crisp.

Serve with roasted peppers and rocket.

BEETROOT & RICOTTA RAVIOLI

RAVIOLI

200G GRADE 'O' PASTA FLOUR
2 EGGS

FILLING

4 COOKED BEETROOTS, GRATED
1 TUB RICOTTA CHEESE
SCATTERING ROSEMARY AND THYME
SALT AND PEPPER

SAUCE

200ML CREAM
100ML WHITE WINE
HANDFUL CHOPPED PARSLEY
2TBSP LEMON JUICE
PEPPER

FOR THE FILLING, mix all ingredients together. To make the ravioli sieve the flour into a bowl or onto a clean surface and crack in the eggs. Gently mix and pull the mixture with your hands until it forms a dough. Once made into a ball, roll out like thin pastry. Divide in half, so you have two sheets.

Then you have to spoon 1tsp amounts of filling on to one sheet 3cm apart in each direction. Once you have filled the sheet, gently brush the edges between fillings with egg, oil or water, then lay another finely rolled sheet of past on top of the first. Cut down in between each spoonful. You can use a fluted pasta cutter, but anything will do from a sharp knife, to a pizza roller. Press edges to seal.

Heat a large pan of lightly salted water to a rolling boil. Cook the ravioli in this for 2-3 minutes, then drain and portion.

For the sauce gently heat white wine to reduce and add cream, then finally lemon, parsley and pepper. Pour over each portion. Serve with semi-dried cherry tomatoes and blanched broad beans.

A COCKTAIL FIT FOR A DUKE

DUKE'S PALATE

50ML CHOSEN SPIRIT
BACARDI 8YR RUM
TANQUERAY 10 GIN
BELVEDERE VODKA
WOODFORD RESERVE

12.5ML LILLET BLANC
5ML GOMME SYRUP
25ML CHAMPAGNE

STIR over cubed ice,
STRAIN into chilled glass and
TOP with champagne.

GARNISH with citron twist
(LEMON WITH GIN OR VODKA, ORANGE
WITH AGED RUM OR BOURBON)

CHEERS to ROB from BROWNS SHEFFIELD bar team, who has created our official 40th Birthday Cocktail. It's a triumph of flexible mixology, we think.

A choice of four quality spirits as the main component mirrors the party mood we're all in. It might be fun to compare and contrast all four alternatives!

The inclusion of champagne adds the perfect celebratory note, too, for this great anniversary.

BACARDI 8 · BELVEDERE VODKA · Tanqueray · WOODFORD RESERVE